THE MAGIC
OF
"SO WHAT"

THE MAGIC
OF
"SO WHAT"

Lt Col (Dr) D.D. Goel (Retd.)

PENTAGON PRESS LLP

First published in 2026
by

PENTAGON PRESS LLP
206, Peacock Lane, Shahpur Jat
New Delhi-110049, India
Contact: 011-26490600

Typeset in Calisto MT, 13 Point
Printed at Thomson Press India Pvt. Ltd.

ISBN 978-81-993527-7-3

www.pentagonpress.in

CONTENTS

PREFACE

Behind every soldier who marches into battle, there stands a silent warrior at home, a mother whose love becomes an unbreakable shield and whose prayers forge an invisible armour. This book is first and foremost dedicated to my mother, the extraordinary woman who gave me life twice, first when she brought me into this world, and then again when she infused me with the strength to live fully, even after I lost my leg.

When the blast shattered my leg, and after several weeks when I was finally sent home on sick leave, I arrived at the railway station. I stepped out of the coach, leaning heavily on my crutches and just one leg. Seeing me like that, helpless yet determined, tore her apart from inside. But without ever letting her pain show, she quietly wiped her tears away and hugged me. Her silent strength at that moment became my beacon of hope, reminding me that even in the hardest of times, love and courage can shine the brightest. Her quiet suffering far away from the battlefield was a powerful testament. When despair whispered that my journey was over, it was her voice that rose above all doubts, thunderous and unwavering, urging me to rise again and again. Her hands, folded in prayer, lifted me higher than any crutch or prosthetic ever could. Her unyielding faith became the fertile soil in which my broken spirit took root and blossomed anew.

Through the long nights of pain and uncertainty, it was her strength that kept the flame of hope burning inside me. Each step I took towards recovery, every challenge I overcame, carried the echoes of her relentless courage and sacrifice. She never once allowed me to believe that my disability defined my destiny.

To my mother, I owe the courage to say, "So what if I have lost a limb? I won't lose my will." Her strength became my strength, her resilience became my armour and her boundless love became the wind beneath my wings, the very reason I chose to fly when the world doubted my ability to walk.

No words can truly capture the depth of gratitude I hold for her. This dedication is a humble attempt to honour her indomitable spirit, a spirit that taught me that even in our darkest hours, love is the greatest source of power, and faith the strongest force of all.

PRELUDE

Warfare changes everything. It's not just about battles and guns, it's about moments that stay with you long after the dust settles, moments of fear, courage, and hope.

During one intense cross-firing at the Line of Control in Kashmir, we got stuck in a narrow gully between steep cliffs. Above us, artillery fire rumbled loudly, shaking the earth beneath our feet. The noise, the threat, and the struggle to survive that day are deeply etched in my memory.

A few weeks later, fate dealt a heavy blow, I lost my leg. But that marked the beginning of a new battle within me, a fight to reclaim my life and spirit.

Two decades later, I returned to Kashmir and visited the very place where I had lost my leg. I climbed the ridge where it all happened, memories rushing in the blast, the pain, and the will to keep going.

At a nearby BSF post, I met Muzammil, a local Kashmiri porter, one of the brave men who had carried me that day. Hearing his story and knowing how he helped save my life gave me a profound sense of closure. It felt as if a cycle had come full circle. Twenty years after that fateful day, here I was, standing where my journey had changed for ever.

But this philosophy of "So what" isn't mine alone. It belongs to everyone who refuses to let setbacks define their story.

Take Anshul, who was boarded out from the Indian Military Academy, a crushing blow for any young cadet's dreams. Most would have seen this as the end of their military aspirations. But Anshul looked at his rejection and said, "So what?" He didn't let one institution's decision limit his potential. Instead, he redirected his determination and later served with distinction in the Royal British Army, proving that dreams don't die, they just find different paths to fulfilment.

Then there's Apurva, who started as a cook in the Indian Army, a role many might consider humble or limiting. But when others saw boundaries, Apurva saw possibilities under unavoidable ups and downs in service. With relentless determination and the courage to dream bigger, he eventually quit and moved to the USA and built a successful diamond business. His journey from an Army kitchen to become an international entrepreneur shows that your starting point doesn't determine your destination.

And Lt Avnish Bajpayee (now Lt Col), who, like me, lost his leg in service to the nation. The surgeons told him his activities would be restricted. But Avnish embraced the "So what" mindset completely. So what if he has one leg? So what if it seemed impossible? Today, he runs full marathons, inspiring thousands with every stride, proving that the human spirit can outrun any physical limitation.

These stories, and countless others like them,

remind us that "So what" isn't just about accepting what happens to us. It's about refusing to accept limitations on what we can become.

This book is about these journeys, battles fought both outside and within, and the simple phrase that kept me moving forward when all else seemed lost: "So what."

It's more than just words. It's a beacon in the darkness, a call to rise again and again. And it belongs to all of us.

CHAPTER I

FROM THE WAR DIARY

Let me take you back to July 2002, to a remote high-altitude outpost about 98 kilometres from Srinagar in Jammu and Kashmir. We were perched at a stunning height of 4,300 metres above sea level on what was once a Pakistani post, captured by us. Because of this, the enemy retaliated fiercely, firing relentless artillery shells and heavy machine-gun bursts from all sides. The enemy was constant, but the harsh mountain weather was no less brutal. The biting cold pierced through every layer, with temperatures plunging well below zero day and night. Out there, the enemy wasn't just across the border, it was the unforgiving terrain and icy winds that tested our endurance every single day. Not far from us at the top was another smaller post, "Point 4444," named after its height. Both posts were under constant attack, day and night, from artillery shells and heavy machine guns. By the grace of God or may be the enemy's poor aiming, not a single bullet or shell hit us. But that continuous assault tested our spirit every moment. Our post stood firm, we swore not to break.

I was a young officer then, full of energy and maybe a little exuberant too. I was eager for action, ready to strike back instead of just sitting and taking fire. My company commander, Major Bahadur Singh, was experienced and careful, but I was waiting for the green signal to launch an attack. I studied the maps carefully, prepared possible attack routes, and even conducted night reconnaissance missions stealthily sneaking out under the cover of darkness to scout the enemy. Every night, I would creep close to the Line of Control to watch the enemy post. I wanted to be ready for the moment we would be ordered to act.

One evening, a radio set message warned us that

the enemy might be planning a BAT action, a Border Action Team attack against our post. These teams are special forces soldiers from the Pakistani Army, often joined by terrorists from groups like Jaish-e-Mohammed and Lashkar-e-Taiba. They launch surprise raids with mortar and artillery cover fire. Hearing this, I knew we might soon have to act.

As a post commander, I started checking every possible path the enemy could use to reach us, as well as our routes for attack or retreat. One night, while making my rounds and thinking over the BAT threat, I stepped outside the bunker to get a better look at the front. I stood in a corner of our fortifications, staring into the darkness at the enemy post. Though protected well, I wanted to be sure there were no blind spots.

That's when I noticed a faint track leading towards the enemy. Partially hidden behind a large boulder that jutted out like a small cliff, it wasn't obvious at first. But once spotted, I realized this could be a hidden route. If I could clearly see the enemy post from there, then someone sneaking along this path could approach undetected. My heart raced. This could be our secret way to strike if we ever got the order. But it could also be a risk if the enemy knew of the path.

I quickly called my team inside and told them what I had found. We decided to scout it immediately that night, despite the occasional shelling. Under the dark sky, I led a small group down the narrow, rocky pass.

We covered about a hundred metres. From that point, the enemy post was clearer and much closer than from our main post. My adrenaline shot up. I whispered to my men that this was our chance to launch an attack if the orders came. But we had to stay alert the same path could be a trap.

Suddenly, the whistling sound and crashing of artillery rounds filled the air, the enemy had resumed shelling over us. We were exposed in a narrow gully between rocky cliffs. One shell there could have been deadly. The roar of the shells was deafening. I knew we had to retreat, and fast.

I signalled to fall back. We moved as trained, the youngest soldier first, followed by the others. But the journey back wasn't easy. Our way was blocked by a six-foot high boulder in that narrow gully, the same one we had jumped over earlier. Now, under a fierce hail of enemy fire, we had to climb it. It was a tough and dangerous climb.

To keep panic from spreading, I stood firm and focused. I made sure every one of my men crossed that boulder safely. Only when the last soldier was clear did I climb it myself, moving as the last man, guiding everyone back. We scrambled up the boulder and raced upward as shells screamed overhead. Fear almost gripped our minds, but we fought to stay calm. In my head, I quietly repeated, almost as if hearing it aloud "So what". So what if it costs me my life? I have a task to complete, to get my men back safe and prepare for what's next.

I encouraged my men out loudly: "Keep moving! Almost there!" and "This is just the beginning! We'll show them soon!" These words, simple as they were, kept our spirits strong.

After what seemed like an endless hour, we reached our post, one by one. I counted every man safely inside and felt immense relief. We had done a successful reconnaissance and safe return under enemy fire.

Back in the bunker, we reviewed what we'd learned. The enemy post was dangerously close and also within reach if we attacked. The path we had discovered was both a chance and a risk it could be our secret way or theirs. We also pinpointed an ideal target area for offensive operations.

With this information, I decided we must deny the enemy the use of that path. The plan was to lay mines (hidden explosives) that would blow up anyone trying to cross. It was a purely defensive move to prevent us from surprise attacks.

We worked quickly and quietly. Mines were placed along the track, making it extremely dangerous for the enemy. As it turned out, the feared raid never came. The enemy had likely realized the route was compromised or had lost the element of surprise.

Soon after, our artillery units responded with heavy fire. Our guns roared, shaking the earth as they struck the enemy post hard. For days, the front was silent, enemy guns fell quiet, pushed back by our might.

This episode taught me how planning, quick decisions, and courage can turn the tide. Instead of panicking, we thought: "So what if it's risky? Let's find a way." By adapting to retreating when needed, we turned the threat into our advantage.

In the Army, I've seen many heroes who live by sheer will and the "So what" spirit. Soldiers learn early to think clearly, even in terrifying moments. That's the true magic of "So what", it lets you fight fear and act decisively.

In our forces, "So what" isn't just word, it's a code. It fuels the fighting spirit, a voice inside saying, "Whatever the obstacle, we will overcome." This attitude helps leaders make hard decisions calmly, whether in battle or in life's daily challenges.

War is chaos, unpredictable and harsh. But "So what" turns hopelessness into just another problem to solve. That night at the post, I lived this truth firsthand.

The power of "So what" goes beyond the battlefield. Soldiers often carry this mindset when they go back and adapt to civilian life, ready to face challenges with calm courage. In any crisis, big or small, they stand firm and say, "So what if it's tough? We'll handle it."

In the great story of the Indian Army's bravery and beyond, "So what" shines bright. It reminds us that no matter how hard things look, we have the power not to be defeated by fear. We face danger, difficulties, and still boldly say, "So what, let's move forward."

This simple phrase carries an unbreakable spirit, the strength to push through tough times and win against all odds.

CHAPTER II

STEPPING TOWARDS A NEW BEGINNING

The journey to a fresh start is never easy. It often has many ups and downs that test our patience and strength. My own journey began when I was thinking of leaving my job as a lecturer. My salary was often delayed, and I had a family to support, including a pregnant wife. As the academic year was ending, I had to seriously think about my future. I started looking for jobs in the private sector, not knowing the journey would be so difficult.

I gave almost a hundred interviews in one month, and none of them worked out. During that time, I survived on *chai* and *vada paav* from wherever I found a tea stall. After each failed interview, I would feel a bit gloomy. But I developed a small routine at the *chaiwala's* stall. I would watch the *chai* being made, hold the warm glass, and take a sip. This became my moment to think. Instead of feeling low, a little voice in my head would say, *"So what!"* That simple thought helped me move on to the next step. It gave me hope and helped me stay positive.

Those tough days slowly made me stronger from within. Even after facing so many rejections, I held on to that simple phrase "So what!" It pushed me forward. I kept hoping and believing that something better would come. And it did come. That same attitude helped me face the biggest challenge of my life, clearing the Service Selection Board (SSB) and joining the Indian Army.

When I went for the SSB, I carried the same mindset: *"So what if I fail? I'll still give my best."* This simple attitude, built through my struggles, made a big difference. In the end, I was selected to serve one of the best organizations in the world.

Looking back, I realize that the "So what!" mindset was not just a way to feel better, it became a way of life. It helped me handle failure, stay calm, and never give up. It taught me that failure is not the end, sometimes, it is just the beginning of something better. Every time I said "So what!" I was taking one step closer to a new opportunity.

"After any event or failure, follow the rule of disengagement, take a moment for yourself before thinking too much (disengage). That small pause can make a big difference."

CHAPTER III

THE MAGIC OF "SO WHAT!"

Life never comes without challenges, be it at home, in career, or in our emotions. Sometimes we are stressed, sometimes de-motivated, and most often, afraid of what others will think. Fear of judgment, fear of failing, or even small embarrassments start building invisible walls around us. We stop trying, stop dreaming, and stop growing.

But here lies the strength of two simple words: "So what!"

Yes, So what! Simple yet powerful enough to shake off self-doubt and silence society's rattle. It is like a tiny shield that makes fears look smaller than they really are.

Why "So What" Works

Think about it. Most of our troubles are not the event itself, but the meaning we give to it. If you fail an exam, lose money in business, or stumble during a speech, what matters more is the incident or the endless worrying that follows?

The moment you say, "So what?" You cut that worry by half.

It's not denial. It's acceptance with courage. *Bas itna hi?*

In India, we often hear people repeating phrases like *"Mere bas ki baat nahin hai"* ("This is not in my control"), or *"Main kya karu?"* Always negative, always self-defeating. When spoken repeatedly, these words become our truth.

"So what" acts like a linguistic switch. Instead of saying "I failed," you end up saying, "I failed…so what? Let me try again." Over time, language builds mindset, mindset builds habits, and habits build life.

Let me share a slice from my own life. Years ago, I ran a small *dhaba* in the bustling lanes of South

Mumbai. Business was steady, but when roadwork blocked our street, customers almost vanished overnight. Every day I saw my team, daily-wage workers, growing anxious as sales dropped and salaries became uncertain.

One evening, with worry on everyone's faces, I gathered them and said, "So what if today you have less work and fewer customers? *Kal phir se nayi subah hogi!* We'll figure it out together."

That "So what" moment became our backbone. It did not magically fix our finances, but it gave us resilience to face each day with fresh hope and unity. Step by step, that attitude pulled us through the crisis.

That's what I mean when I talk about the magic of "So what." It transforms stress into courage, and despair into perseverance even in Mumbai's chaos.

Of course, "So what" is not a licence to escape responsibility. If you miss office deadlines and casually say "So what," you're making a fool of yourself. The *mantra* is not for laziness, it is for courage, for being upright.

Used rightly, "So what" doesn't avoid problems. It says, "Yes, the problem is real. So what? I will still stand, still try, still move forward."

Whether it is starting a business, speaking on stage, or simply telling someone your honest opinion – the first barrier is fear. Fear of 'what ifs'.

The next time your mind stops you with thoughts like, "What if I fail? What if they laugh? What if I don't succeed?" just answer back with "So what?"

This one counter-question is enough to put you back in charge of your life.

I remember when I got married without a secure job. Everyone warned me, it's risky, wait till you're settled." I replied in my heart, "So what, together we will build it." And life unfolded exactly the same way. That conviction became my silent prayer and guiding compass.

"So what" is not just personal. In a team or family, these words can unite everyone. Suppose a project doesn't meet its target. Instead of blaming each other, if the group collectively says, "So what? Let's find another way," energy suddenly replaces exhaustion.

It is more than a phrase, it is a spirit of resilience.

Society keeps telling us what we "should" do, which career is worthy, what age is ideal for marriage, what defines success. Somewhere, we get trapped in these invisible chains.

But when you whisper, "So what," you take control back. You stop living somebody else's story and start writing your own.

It's not rebellion without direction, it's freedom with responsibility.

The magic of "So what" lies in its simplicity. Anyone can use it, a student before an exam, a mother handling family stress, a businessman facing setbacks, or a youngster silenced by society's judgments.

"So what" doesn't make problems vanish, but it makes us larger than the problem.

It is hope over fear, action over paralysis, and courage over doubt.

From this day, whenever adversity knocks at your door, welcome it with a smile and whisper back, "So what."

CHAPTER IV

THE "SO WHAT" MAGIC IN AVOIDING THINGS

As soon as I announced the title of my next book, '*The Magic of So What*', my phone started buzzing. My friends enjoyed this situation immensely. One even sent me a voice message, chuckling, "Boss, you're writing on 'So What'? Now this is a topic you simply must cover!" He then narrated a delightfully familiar scene from home. "In my house, my wife turns 'So what' into her secret weapon. Forget motivational *mantras Yaar*, she casually uses it to avoid every bit of advice I give her!"

Picture this:

I gently caution her, "Cut down on sweets, you might gain weight."

Without missing a beat: "So what."

I remind her, "Food is burning on the gas!"

She shrugs, "So what, *tumhi ko toh khana hai*!" (You're the one who has to eat it anyway!)

I suggest, "Maybe read a book, broaden your mind."

"So what."

I urge, "Don't leave things for the last minute, it's not good!"

She flashes a grin: "So what."

Basically, if I say anything from finance to fitness, cooking to career, I get the classic shut-it-down, "So what." Our children have started using it too. Now the whole house is a 'So what' party!

But here's the twist. This magic word, which ends all family discussions, vanishes when real challenges pop up:

Ask her to walk a little farther than usual, suddenly "So what" is gone, she'll negotiate, sulk, and call me heartless!

Lost the house keys? You'd expect, "So what, let's get a duplicate." But no, we have a full-on manhunt.

Shopping for a sari? Will she pick anything? Not a chance! hours go by, and "So what, *koi bhi chalega*" (anything will do)? Nope!

It's funny how "So what" becomes a convenient shield for brushing off your spouse's advice yet disappears when adversity calls. This is the *desi* paradox of "So what" the double-edged sword of Indian households.

This story reveals the true heart of the *mantra*: "So what" can be a lazy excuse for not listening, or a powerful *mantra* for facing actual challenges, it's all about how we use it.

If only we used "So what" at the right time! Imagine:

Lost something? "So what, I'll find another way."

Got to walk a little extra? "So what, I'll get fitter."

Plans went wrong. "So what, *kal naya din hoga*!" (Tomorrow will be a new day!)

The real power of "So what" is in making us bold, not dismissive. It's not for dodging advice or avoiding the tough stuff, it's for embracing life's uncertainties with a smile and a shrug.

So, the next time you're caught between a burnt *sabzi* and a missed deadline, try the real "So what". You'll discover it's not just a reply, it's an attitude shift that could turn your ordinary day into a tale worth telling.

CHAPTER V

I WROTE TO FIND OUT WHAT I KNOW

Let me confess something that might surprise you. I never sat down to write my first book because "I had it all figured out." Far from it! Writing for me, has always been a journey full of surprises, half treasure hunt, half wrestling match with my own mind.

People think authors have some magic light bulb moment, but the truth is, most days I sat in front of a blank page thinking, "Boss, what do I have to say?" For over a year, my life was a mad juggle, managing office, running errands for my ill mother, tending to a prosthetic leg that sometimes felt like its own high-maintenance family member (trust me, you haven't truly multitasked until you've nursed a blister on your leg while chasing an idea that threatens to escape). To make things more interesting or foolish, I signed up for a half marathon after 12 years of losing a limb, trying to jog both on the road and in my thoughts!

With so many plates spinning, who has time to write? Still, that nagging itch to tell my story just wouldn't leave me alone. But every time I picked up a pen (or laptop), one question haunted me: "What should I actually write about?" And then, its elder brother joined in: "How should I write it?" Those two questions became my personal demon duo, ensuring my book remained an eternal "Work in progress."

For almost two years, I played the world's longest round of consultation discussing with friends, family, mentors, even auto rickshaw drivers if they looked philosophical enough! Everyone gave well-meaning advice, but nobody could silence my main critic, my own mind.

Then came one ordinary Tuesday, when disappointment and frustration reached boiling point. That's when something clicked. I looked in the mirror and said aloud, "So what!" – So what if I don't know how to start? So what if my writing isn't perfect? So what if nobody reads it? The moment I gave myself that command, the wall vanished.

I discovered the "So what" attitude isn't just about facing big storms. Sometimes it's about shrugging off small clouds that cast long shadows.

With the weight off my shoulders, ideas that were trapped inside for years finally trickled out. I made a plan, simple, stepwise, Indian *jugaad* style. In just six months, words turned into chapters, chapters into a book, and that book found its own journey in the world.

The proudest moment? Watching the Chief of the Indian Army launch my book, knowing all the struggles, second-guessing, and occasional blisters had finally led to this day. Reviews poured in, my phone wouldn't stop ringing, and all I could think was, "Was it really just my self-doubt that held me back this long?"

This journey taught me more about myself than any biography ever could. The biggest hurdles weren't "out there", not lack of time, not lack of ideas, not even the prosthetic leg. My real roadblock was always between my two ears.

Writing became my personal deep dive, my way of finding what was truly inside me. The "So what" mantra didn't remove my problems, but it reminded me that I could face them. Every page I wrote echoed this truth: The only chain stopping us is the one we create in our mind.

So if you're waiting for the "perfect" moment, trust me, just say "So what!" and begin. Maybe, just maybe, you'll discover what you're made of along the way.

"It's only your thought which stops you."

CHAPTER VI

A SYMPHONY OF RESILIENCE: THE STORY OF LT AVNISH BAJPAI

The Indian Military Academy in Dehradun is surrounded by beautiful mountains, but let's be honest, life there is no holiday. It's a place where tomorrow's officers are tested every single day with strict discipline and tough training. Take Avnish Bajpai another Gentlemen Cadet whose dreams were as high as the Himalayas around him. Every morning, Avnish was out there giving his hundred per cent, running obstacle courses, sweating it out in drills determined to join the Para Special Forces.

In the Academy, the friendship and brotherhood made every hardship easier to bear.

After months of non-stop rigorous training, the big day arrived, filling the choice of Arms, the day Gentlemen Cadets opt for the regiments they want to join as officers. But, as luck would have it, things didn't go as planned for Avnish. That year, the Para Special Forces had only a handful of openings, and Avnish just missed making the cut. He was heartbroken, anyone would be. But in true fauji style, he shrugged, "So what!" and accepted 'The Infantry'. Instead of sulking, he grabbed the next chance with both hands. That simple attitude to not let one missed dream stop you said everything.

Soon after getting commissioned, life threw him a curveball that would shake anyone. In the spring of 2011, while on a military exercise, Lt Avnish suffered a casualty and lost his left leg. Unimaginable, right? One day he was fighting fit in his regiment, the next, he loses a limb. It was the sort of thing that could bring a mountain down, let alone a person. That year, I moved to Pune and got a new crimson-red Royal Enfield bike, picturing thrilling rides ahead. I never guessed that bike would become a symbol of hope for Lt Avnish too.

After the casualty, Lt Avnish was shifted to the Command Hospital in Pune for treatment and rehab. Multiple surgeries and then day after day of gruelling physical therapy, learning to walk on an artificial leg from scratch. The hospital's Artificial Limb Centre became his home away from home. That place was full of tough soldiers who had seen their share of battles now they were fighting their hardest war, to regain their lives. The sound of therapy sessions echoed in the corridors, a mix of pain and determination.

In rehab, Lt Avnish wasn't alone. Many injured soldiers, each with their own scars and stories, bonded together. They laughed, joked, inspired, and pushed each other through the pain. For Avnish, his prosthetic leg became a badge of stubborn pride, a sign that he wouldn't let Fate decide his limits. With every step, it was as if he told the world, "This injury won't control my life." It wasn't just about walking, it was about fighting back the body and mind.

One evening, during my visit to the hospital to meet him, I saw something wonderful. Avnish wasn't just another patient, he was an example for everyone. His grit and spirit turned him into an inspiration. Anyone struggling could look at him and feel, "If this guy can fight, so can I." Avnish had become living proof: you can choose to be the hero of your own story.

I decided to invite him over for dinner at my Pune home. The evening was peaceful, the lawn glowing in the sunset. There, sitting with *chai* and biscuits, Avnish opened up about his dreams. Despite all that had happened, he was still dreaming big. That night, out of the blue, I challenged him to a sprint across my lawn. At first, he hesitated, understandable, with a new prosthetic leg. I smiled and said, "So what! Let's see." He agreed, and together we ran those 40 metres, laughing breathlessly at the finish line. That race wasn't about speed. It was about breaking invisible chains. For Avnish, it was his first run after his injury, a small sprint, a huge victory.

But the evening wasn't done. Next, I led him to my bright red Royal Enfield outside. "Take her for a spin," I urged. The bike, a symbol of adventure, now stood for a new kind of courage. It's not easy to ride a heavy Bullet with a prosthetic leg! Avnish wavered, but I cheered him on, "So what if it's tough? You've got this." He climbed on, fired up the bike, and rode off down the quiet Pune roads. He came back, helmet in hand, eyes shining. That short ride was a declaration: "Nothing will hold me back."

From then, I called him fighter Avnish Bajpai and he truly deserved it. Where others may have given up, he turned every obstacle into new strength. For him, "Why me?" was replaced by "So what, I'll do it anyway!" Every challenge was a rung on his ladder upwards.

Lt Avnish soon received his final prosthetic leg and left for his new posting, ready to face the world once again. I remained in Pune, carrying on with my duties.

Then, life brought its own test. In January 2014, I lost my mother. The pain was deep, and my heart was heavier than ever before. In the midst of that grief, I decided to honour her in the best way I knew by running the Mumbai Half Marathon. It had been 12 long years since I lost my left leg, but this time, every step was filled with love for my mother. This run would be my tribute to her, a way to tell myself that no loss could break the human spirit. That day I finished the 21-km half marathon in two hours and twenty minutes offering a befitting honour to my mum.

As I ran through the streets of Mumbai that day, emotions overwhelmed me. My head was down, lost in thought, just following the road, when suddenly I noticed someone else running with an artificial limb. To my surprise, it was Captain Avnish Bajpai, running his first half marathon, 21 kilometres on a prosthetic leg. For a moment, my world stood still. There we were two soldiers, both on artificial legs, running side by side in the middle of that massive crowd. For us, it wasn't just a race, it was about telling the world, "Nothing is impossible."

But what truly touched me was Avnish's spirit. He didn't stop with that half marathon. A year later, in December 2015, I saw him again, this time at the Delhi Marathon. But now, he wasn't running 21 kilometres, he was running a full marathon, all 42 kilometres. Just imagine, this is the same Avnish who, after losing his leg, once sprinted only 40 metres with me for the first time, hesitantly and with doubt. Now, with grit, hope, and his "So what" attitude, he was conquering one of the toughest runs on a prosthetic leg. That's incredible, even for those with both legs.

For Avnish, "So what" became more than a phrase, it became his Battle Cry, his way of tackling every challenge life threw at him. And after that, he didn't stop, he went on to try skydiving, scuba diving, and more. Unstoppable, fearless, and truly inspiring.

Today, Lt Col Avnish Bajpai isn't just a name, he's an inspiration, inside and outside the military. His story proves that if you're willing to say "So what!" to life's biggest setbacks, you can climb heights no one thought possible. His courage is a song for anyone who's ever faced tough times.

The Indian Military Academy teaches more than just drills, it shapes minds for life. It's not only medals that make a soldier, it's these unspoken battles and comebacks. Every time I see that red Royal Enfield, I remember that night in Pune, and how one "So what!" turned a defeat into victory.

CHAPTER VII

RISING ABOVE THE LIMITS OTHERS SET FOR YOU

It is often said that being pushed into a corner during difficult times does not change anything. However, I believe real transformation happens when you are faced with adversity and confront it with a strong "So what" attitude.

During my tenure as an instructor at the Indian Military Academy (IMA) in Dehradun, I met a Gentleman Cadet named Anshul. He had a dream of becoming an officer in the Indian Army, and from the beginning, he stood out as someone special. Getting into the IMA itself is an enormous challenge where you must pass the tough Service Selection Board (SSB) exams and medical tests, and only then do you get the chance to train at the Academy. Even after that, you must clear all the demanding physical and academic tests during training to finally be commissioned as an officer.

Before joining the IMA, he had already walked a difficult path, he attempted the SSB four times. Each time, he faced rejection. But he never once thought of giving up. He was resilient then, and he remained resilient later as well. With unwavering determination and an unshakeable belief in himself, he finally cleared the SSB in his fourth attempt. He joined the Indian Military Academy, but his journey was not smooth. He struggled with one particular physical test that was mandatory for all cadets. He gave it his all but unfortunately failed the test and was "relegated," meaning he had to repeat a six-month term of training. In fact, he was relegated twice, each time adding a six-month delay to his progress. After multiple attempts and still not passing that crucial test, the Academy had to make the hard decision to board him out, which meant he could no longer continue at the IMA. It was a tough moment after coming so far, he had to leave without achieving his dream of graduating as an officer.

At that critical moment, I felt it was my duty to encourage him. I saw the disappointment on his face, knowing how much effort he had put in. Before he left, I told him some simple but meaningful words: "So what, my friend? Life doesn't stop here. Wherever you go next, strive for excellence." I wanted him to know that one setback did not mean the end of his journey.

Anshul took these words to heart. His journey after leaving the Academy truly showed the power of the "So what" spirit. Instead of giving up, he pushed forward with determination. He did not see his failure at the IMA as the destination. He moved on and channelized his energy into something new. He went on to acquire higher qualifications and moved to the UK, where he worked as a learning technologist at Cambridge University. This was a huge achievement and an important turning point in his life.

Even after reaching Cambridge, Anshul's ambition did not stop. A few years later, he set an even higher goal for himself, to serve in the Royal British Army. The process was another rigorous challenge with SSB interviews and tests. True to his character, Anshul gave it his best shot. "Let's see," he thought, "so what if it doesn't work? I will still give it a try!" With that mindset, he cleared the Service Selection Board, but this time for the Royal British Army. He went on to serve in the Territorial Army in the UK, a fresh start that was not just a career change but a testament to his refusal to be limited by past setbacks.

Today, Anshul continues to serve with pride in the Territorial Army of the Royal British Army, carrying the same fire and discipline that once fueled his dream at the Indian Military Academy. With every parade, every command, and every mission, he stands tall as a symbol of perseverance and commitment. His journey from facing rejection in IMA Dehradun to wearing the uniform in a foreign land is not just a personal victory, it's a story of never giving up on oneself. Through his dedication,

Anshul has earned not only the respect of his comrades but also the satisfaction of knowing that his struggles became the foundation of his success.

What makes Anshul's story so inspiring is his refusal to treat any setback as the end. Each time something didn't go as planned, he treated it as an opportunity to grow rather than a permanent failure. He had an unyielding belief in himself. Whenever a challenge arose, he essentially said to himself, "So what if I failed? I'll try again or I'll try something else." This attitude turned his setbacks into stepping stones. His journey shows that failures are not roadblocks, they are just milestones on the way to success.

Life is a fascinating journey with countless opportunities waiting for us. We don't always know when luck or success will come our way. Our dreams might be closer than we think, but it's hard to be sure. What we *can* do is to stay consistent and resilient. We must keep working towards our goals and not lose hope when things don't go our way. In fact, when we face obstacles, simply saying "So what" can be a powerful way to remind ourselves to keep going. With that unwavering determination, we can navigate the ups and downs of life. Every challenge we meet with resilience is another step that brings us closer to achieving our aspirations.

CHAPTER VIII

QUE SERA SERA

Many people spend too much time worrying about things that may never happen. They worry over money troubles, fret about career problems, or imagine the worst-case scenarios. This kind of constant worry eats away at our peace and happiness, making life heavier than it needs to be. The saying *"Que sera, sera"*, which means "Whatever will be, will be," reminds us not to waste energy worrying about the future. Instead, it encourages us to accept life as it comes and face whatever challenges or opportunities arise.

One great example of this calm acceptance mixed with fierce determination is the story of Apurva Chatterji.

Apurva came from a proud family with a history of serving the nation. His maternal grandfather was a freedom fighter. As a child, Apurva was deeply inspired by stories of sacrifice and bravery. He grew up watching men and women in uniform and heard tales of courage, loyalty, and duty. It sparked a fire in him to one day wear the uniform and serve the country with pride.

Like many young boys, Apurva dreamed of joining the Indian Army as an officer. However, life didn't follow a straight path. Instead, he first got a job in the Army as a *khansama*, which means cook. This was not the officer's role he had imagined, but working in an Army kitchen brought him close to the heart of Army life. Every day, he moved among disciplined officers, watched the drills, and understood the dedication needed on the field. His dream never dimmed, it only grew stronger as he learned more about what it meant to serve.

During this time, I got to know Apurva at the Army gym, where he was responsible for opening and closing the gym as per scheduled timings. We spoke often, and I could see his craving to achieve more. I shared with him tips on how to clear the tough Service Selection Board (SSB) exam and strongly encouraged him to continue his education alongside his duties. I suggested that he enrol in a distance-learning post-graduate program, so he could gain qualifications while still working. Apurva took the advice seriously and completed his post-graduation while still working in the Army kitchen, an impressive feat of commitment and time management.

Things were finally moving in a good direction for Apurva, but life had another test waiting. A senior JCO (Junior Commissioned Officer) at his office started creating unnecessary conflicts. At first, it was small disagreements, but soon it turned into bullying. This senior JCO really made Apurva's work life miserable, turning the environment toxic. Every day brought stress that weighed heavily on Apurva's spirit. He was working hard, doing his best to prepare for his future, but this harassment was beyond his control. It clouded his happiness and hope.

One evening, I heard a knock on my door. To my surprise, it was Apurva. His eyes were wet, his face worn out. He spoke honestly about the harassment, the unhappiness, and how he felt like quitting. It was heartbreaking to hear. I listened carefully but didn't rush to offer advice. Instead, I told him to give me a day to think about it, and we would talk again at the gym.

That night, I weighed all the options, the pros and cons of staying and fighting versus quitting and seeking new paths. The next day, I told Apurva that if the situation was hurting him so much, it was okay to walk away. No one deserves to be bullied or miserable at work. Walking away wasn't giving up, sometimes it is the bravest step. Apurva trusted me and decided to resign and return home, taking back control of his life.

Even though quitting brought immediate relief, the future suddenly felt uncertain. Without a clear plan, Apurva felt anxious. During this period, he often called me, seeking guidance and reassurance. I became a mentor and brother figure to him during those testing times. I encouraged him to apply for a passport and consider job opportunities abroad, a place where he could start afresh and find new doors open to him. The world is full of possibilities, and sometimes, they lie beyond our borders.

Apurva listened. He got his passport and began exploring options overseas.

Fate smiled on him when a friend of his father mentioned some job opportunities abroad. What began as uncertainty soon turned into a new path. Apurva remembered the "So what" philosophy. "So what if this isn't my original plan? I'll give it a try!" With that fearless attitude, he decided to go for a course in diamond cutting in the United Kingdom. This was a sharp turn from his dream of being an Army officer, but his open mind and willingness to try new things gave him courage.

In the UK, Apurva enrolled in the course and threw himself into mastering the craft of cutting and polishing diamonds, a skill demanding immense precision and patience. After completing the course, his efforts bore fruit when he secured a job at a prestigious diamond store. From cooking in the Army kitchen to handling world-class jewels, Apurva had rewritten his story in incredible ways. He stayed in touch with me and shared the pride and joy of his achievements. The world he once only dreamed of was now real.

By 2007, Apurva's path took him even further, to the stunning islands of Jamaica. There, he worked in the high-end jewellery business, a tropical paradise far removed from his humble beginnings. No longer in an apron, he dressed sharp and thrived amid the glitz and glamour. In Jamaica, every day was a new adventure meeting people from all over the world, learning the trade deeply, and making a name for himself.

Apurva's natural ability to connect with people and lead helped him flourish. He ran jewellery seminars that attracted top clients from all over the world. And his journey didn't stop. He even set up his own diamond outlet on a cruise ship, travelling across oceans while doing what he loved. Sailing to exotic destinations, carrying a big smile and that fearless "So what" spirit, he truly lived life on his own terms.

Through all these twists and turns, Apurva discovered one crucial truth: real growth happens when you step out of your comfort zone and face challenges head-on. When faced with something scary or unknown, his answer was always "So what, let's give it a shot." This mindset opened doors to opportunities that fear or hesitation would have kept closed.

From a humble *khansama(cook)* in an Army kitchen to a shining star in the international diamond world, Apurva's journey is extraordinary. It's proof that when you believe in yourself, take risks, and say "So what" to obstacles, life makes room for you to shine. His trust in the unknown led him to unexpected success.

In the grand symphony of life, Apurva's melody is clear and inspiring: believe in yourself, take bold steps, and leave worries behind. Step by step, your ladder to success will rise, just keep saying, "Que sera sera."

CHAPTER IX

WHEN COVID-19 CAME KNOCKING

March 2020. The world had gone mad. COVID-19 was all everyone talked about, on TV, whatsapp forwards, family conversations. Fear and anger ruled the day. People were scared of the virus and furious about lockdowns, disruptions, and each other's behaviour.

In my uniformed job, I was meeting soldiers, officers, civilians, lots of people. I knew the risks but tried to stay careful. Still, fate had other plans. During the first wave, I started feeling unwell.

For three days, I brushed it off. Just a cough,

nothing serious. But by the fourth day, I couldn't deny it anymore. Off to the military hospital I went, and by evening, boom. Positive!

My phone wouldn't stop ringing after the news spread. Officers checking on me, family worried sick. Around 7:00 p.m. the duty medical officer called: "Sir, get ready. COVID ambulance will pick you up within the hour."

COVID ambulance! Those two words sent a chill down my spine.

At 10:00 p.m. I was still waiting. When the ambulance finally arrived, I climbed in with my small bag. The medical staff looked like astronauts in their PPE suits, head to toe white plastic. That sight really drove home how serious this was.

I said goodbye to my family, trying to sound brave. "Don't worry, I'll be fine. But I could see the fear in their eyes.

In the ambulance, it was just me, my thoughts, and the steady hum of the engine. My body ached, my cough wouldn't quit. As we drove through empty streets for what felt like hours, my mind went to dark places. What if I never come home? What if this is it?

Then something snapped inside me. Why are you thinking like this? What good will it do? I remembered my training, staying cool under pressure. I shifted focus, let me think about how to handle this. I'll listen to the doctors, fight this like any other battle.

Meanwhile, the ambulance kept moving from hospital to hospital. Each stop, the paramedic would hop out, come back shaking his head in disappointment. No beds available. The co-driver apologetically explained they were trying their best. What if we don't find a place at all?

That's when my military training kicked in. "When the going gets tough, the tough get going!" tough times make tough soldiers. I kept repeating this to myself, along with another phrase: "Will see". Will see this through, whatever happens.

To my civilian friends reading this, inside each of you, there is a soldier. Not the uniform-wearing kind, but the resilient, brave part of your personality that can face hardships. The courage, discipline, and endurance of a soldier exist in everyone. You just need to awaken it when life gets tough.

Finally, around 2 a.m. we found a bed. And get this, it was in the Artificial Limb Centre, the same place where I'd learned to walk again with my prosthetic leg in 2002. Walking into that familiar space felt surreal. The beds that once helped people with new artificial limbs were now treating COVID patients.

The virus hit me hard. Every muscle ached, my eyes burned, I felt completely drained. Simple tasks like changing clothes felt like climbing Everest. But in that moment, I made a conscious choice, I would not let my mind spiral into "what if" scenarios. I'd focus on the present, one moment, one breath at a time.

The ward was packed, nearly 50 patients crammed wherever there was space. The air felt heavy, almost toxic. It was like being stuck in a sealed container full of germs and being told to breathe normally for weeks.

Soon, the news I dreaded came: my family had also tested positive. Now I wasn't just a patient, I was a husband, father, and son trying to keep others calm. Ironically, even though they were sick, they worried more about me than themselves.

From my hospital bed, I coordinated their care, arranging groceries, medicines, even making sure our pet would be looked after. The authorities allowed them to isolate at home instead of a quarantine centre because of our pet. Small relief.

Days blended into nights. Patients came and went from beds around me. Seeing these people recover and leave gave me hope, but also made me anxious. When will it be my turn?

One day, a new patient arrived, a 68-year-old retired officer, clearly scared. After he settled in, I struck up a conversation. He'd been ill for three days. I told him gently, "Sir, don't worry. You've crossed three days already. Tomorrow's your fourth, once you get past that, you're on the path to recovery. I've seen older patients with more complications walk out healthy. Just hold on one more day."

The relief in his eyes was instant like someone had thrown him a lifeline.

By morning, miracle of miracles, he tested negative. He was discharged on his fifth day. Before leaving, he thanked me, saying my words had helped him keep hope alive.

That experience showed me the transformative power of positivity. About a month later, it was finally my turn. I walked out of that hospital, thinner, weaker, but healthy. Throughout the illness, one *mantra* echoed in my mind: "So what, this too shall pass." And it did pass.

Looking back, mental strength played a huge role in recovery. The "So what" attitude, acknowledging difficulty but refusing to be overwhelmed was my guiding light. It not only helped my recovery but seemed to help others too. A little encouragement can create ripples of hope.

During any crisis, health, personal or professional, your mindset matters as much as medicine. When anxiety creeps in, pause and breathe deeply. When anger flares, count backward from twenty. When fear strikes, ask yourself: What is the worst-case scenario?" Clearly define the worst possible outcome and you will realize it is less catastrophic and manageable. But most importantly, remember the magic of "So what." Instead of thinking "this is unbearable", try "So what if this is tough? I'll face it, and this too, shall pass."

Because it always does,

CHAPTER X

REVISITING KASHMIR: COMPLETING THE CYCLE

While I was serving as an instructor at the National Defence Academy, leading a purposeful tenure of nearly two and a half years, a call came from Army Headquarters that changed everything. They asked if I would be interested getting posted to Kashmir. For me, this was the chance of a lifetime, one I couldn't afford to miss. With a broad grin, I nodded without hesitation.

Since 2019, Kashmir was going through turbulent times. Someone had recommended my name to be part of the ongoing operations there. Before the call from Army Headquarters, a General Officer Commanding of a division from Kashmir himself had called to ask if I was willing to come back and serve. That was the time my heart was filled with a strange mix of excitement and emotion, I accepted willingly.

A few months later, I was back in Kashmir. The moment I arrived, memories crashed down. I found myself near the very cantonment where twenty years ago, I had been evacuated and treated at the 92 Base Hospital after losing my leg. The flood of memories was overwhelming. Within weeks of getting posted, I was allotted a house just behind 92 Base Hospital, a place spoken of with reverence. There's a saying about that hospital that if a patient arrives with just a weak pulse, they will surely walk out hale and hearty from there. It's the busiest hospital in the country, handling casualties from all over North and South Kashmir.

Any time I heard a helicopter land on the cantonment helipad, I would ask if any casualties had arrived. If it was someone like me, someone who had lost a limb, I made sure to visit him the next day. I became a beacon of hope for those young soldiers picking up the pieces of their shattered lives. Their questions opened a window into their fears: "Will I be able to ride a Royal Enfield again Sir?" I smiled and showed them pictures of me riding a Bullet, Paragliding, living life to the fullest. And slowly, I saw a ray of hope ignite in their eyes.

Officially, my role was part of the perception management team. Our mission was to bring normalcy to Kashmir by changing mindsets starting with our own people. I was heavily involved in programs designed to counsel radicalized youth and guide them back to society through constructive livelihoods. Working closely with the Director General of Police JK and my headquarters, we aimed to heal communities torn apart by conflict.

During my tenure, I met over 350 misguided youth, many radicalized, overground workers (OGWs) and surrendered terrorists. I walked into homes, community halls, counselled, listened, and gave hope. Supporting their return to normal life was exhausting, there were no breaks, no days off. For almost three years, I travelled nearly 38 villages across Kashmir, connecting with people, families, and young lives desperate for a second chance. Many of them agreed with my ideas, they embraced jobs, learned skills, and chose peace over weapons.

It was during that time I met a senior brigadier, the Brigade Commander in Gurez, the very place where I had lost my leg two decades earlier. I asked him if I could visit the site of my injury one last time. The Brigadier was gracious and promised he'd arrange it. A few weeks later, he told me to come over.

It was 4th October 2022, I made the journey back to Gurez. The next day, I climbed the ridge where I had crossed the Line of Control twenty years ago. My riflemen who accompanied me, warned me to keep low, wary of possible enemy fire. But I said, "Today, nothing will happen. This is personal." Standing there, I could hear the echoes, the blast, the screams, the pain I endured. Memories flooded my mind.

After a quiet moment, I made my way back

down, stopping first at a Border Security Force (BSF) post. The inspector in charge, Mr. Meena offered tea, snacks, and an unexpected revelation. Earlier that day, Muzammil had visited the post to drop off a small generator. As he saw a few of us moving up the mountain, he casually asked the inspector who was climbing to the top. Mr. Meena told him that an officer was visiting the location where he had lost his leg twenty years ago. On hearing this, Muzammil immediately said he wanted to meet me. When I met him, my heart skipped. Muzammil had been one of the locals who had carried me that fateful day. I had always wondered what exactly happened on those mountainside trails, and here was a man who might hold the answers.

He told me, "Sir, when I heard an officer lost a leg, I was guiding soldiers and a medical aid team from the base towards you to help you. In the rush, the medical officer, Col Bidhan, fainted due to the dipping temperature and altitude. I gave him a salt cube and saved his life. We almost forgot about you. When you were carried down, you were conscious, fighting pain, determined that you were going to live and come back to the battalion. I led your team to the main road, about four hours away. After getting you to the ambulance, I returned to my village in the early morning."

Muzammil said something that shook me deeply: "Even today, despite helicopters and advanced equipment, if someone was injured where you were, rescue would be nearly impossible." I felt this was no coincidence but perhaps divine intervention. The freezing weather that day slowed my blood loss and infection, the alternate route Muzammil guided us on, and the care of brave men, it all combined to save my life that day.

That day was 22nd October 2002. And meeting Muzammil on 5th October 2022 was like closing a circle, finally getting answers to questions I had carried for twenty years.

My second journey to Kashmir was purposeful. It was the magic of "So what" that gave me the strength to return to that mountain ridge, confront my past, and find peace.

CHAPTER XI

THE TEST OF DETERMINATION AND COURAGE

In the early months of 2022, while I was serving in the beautiful yet challenging terrain of Kashmir, I walked into General Roopesh Mehta's office with a simple request for leave. When he asked the reason, I casually mentioned, "Sir, I want to go and learn skiing." Instead of just signing the leave application like any other routine request, General Mehta looked at me thoughtfully and challenged me to make this vacation truly meaningful. "Why not do something that will inspire others?" he asked.

After some brainstorming and heart-to-heart discussions, we came up with an idea that would change lives forever: use this time to train a group of specially-abled young people in skiing. The very thought gave me goose bumps. Imagine the impact showing the world that physical limitations need not hold you back from conquering mountains, literally and figuratively. This wasn't just about skiing, it was about breaking barriers and creating hope where there was none.

And so, the hunt began for volunteers. Finding them wasn't a walk in the park. We were looking for young people who had disabilities and who were also willing to take on the challenge of skiing, something even fully abled people find daunting. It was like asking someone to climb Everest when they'd never seen a hill. We reached out through friends, colleagues, social media, local contacts, and various networks. For two long months, we made calls, met families, explained our vision, and faced countless rejections. Some parents were worried about safety, others couldn't believe their children could actually ski.

After persistent efforts and countless conversations, we finally found our warriors, six specially abled youths from Kashmir who were not just willing but eager to embark on this adventure. Each conversation with their families was emotional. Parents oscillated between pride and fear, hope and worry. We assured them, and the authorities organizing the training, that we would take every possible precaution to keep their children safe. We wanted everyone to feel confident that this journey, though challenging, would be transformative, not tragic.

With preparations in place, hearts full of determination, and prayers from families, the D-day arrived on 4th March 2022.

On that crisp morning, in the heart of the majestic Himalayas at Gulmarg, I stood with my six new teammates, six young souls from Kashmir, each carrying their own story of struggle, each with a different disability, yet united by an unbreakable spirit. The snow-capped peaks around us seemed to whisper, "are you ready for what's coming?" We were about to embark on a journey that would test not just our physical strength but reveal the incredible power of the human spirit that resided within each of us.

Let me introduce you to these six rock stars, each with their own personality and charm:

Gowhair Ahmad Ganaie, the eternal optimist, always wearing a smile that could light up even the coldest Kashmir morning. His laughter was infectious, and even in the toughest moments, he'd find a reason to chuckle.

Umar Salam, the thoughtful philosopher of our group. Quiet, serious, but with eyes that sparkled with determination. He analyzed every move, every technique, and approached challenges with the wisdom of someone much older.

Abdul Rehman Mir, our happy-go-lucky spirit, the one who turned every setback into a story worth telling. His carefree attitude masked a steel-like determination that would surprise everyone.

Rafiq, mature beyond his teenage years, tough

as nails. Life had already tested him in ways most people couldn't imagine, and he wore his resilience like armour.

Musaib Rashid, the quiet achiever who believed in letting his efforts speak louder than words. He worked twice as hard as anyone else and never complained, not even once.

Syeed Nazir, the youngest of our group, mischievous and full of the kind of energy that makes you believe anything is possible. His playful nature kept our spirits high even during the most challenging moments.

On the evening of 3rd March 2022, we all gathered at the legendary High Altitude Warfare School (HAWS) in Gulmarg. Just being there was overwhelming. HAWS isn't just any training institute, it's where heroes are created. This prestigious institution of the Indian Army specializes in mountain and snow warfare training, where our soldiers learn to survive and fight in conditions that would break ordinary men. It was established in 1948 and officially named HAWS in 1962, this school has a glorious history and has contributed significantly and successfully in missions during the Kargil war and countless other operations.

Usually, only seasoned soldiers get to train at this hallowed ground. The fact that we were allowed to use their world-class facilities for our skiing training made us feel incredibly special, like we were part of something much bigger than ourselves, something that would inspire generations to come.

The setting was nothing short of magical, but the conditions were as harsh as they were beautiful. Winter in the Himalayas doesn't just test you, it tries to break you. The air was so cold it felt like needles piercing our lungs with every breath. Icy winds cut across our faces like sharp blades, and temperatures plummeted way below zero, bone-chilling, doesn't even begin to describe it.

For my team, the cold presented a double challenge. All the boys, including me, were amputees. Some had lost a leg above the knee, others below, and some both. They all used prosthetic limbs. In such brutal weather, the leg that's amputated becomes completely numb, making the condition worse where you might not feel if there is an injury or if something is wrong with the prosthetics. We had to constantly check that our prosthetic legs were properly aligned and secure. If they shifted even slightly and we couldn't feel it due to the numbness, it could cause painful cuts or skin tears without us realizing it immediately.

The mornings were the worst. Waking up in those freezing barracks, feeling the stiffness in our bodies, seeing our breath form clouds in the icy air, it took tremendous willpower just to get out of bed. Yet, every single morning, we looked at each other, took a deep breath, and prepared to face another day of challenges because we had come here with a purpose, and that purpose was bigger than our comfort, bigger than our fears.

Right from day one, we faced our biggest nemesis, mastering skiing in conditions that would test even the most experienced athletes. Think about how challenging it is for a regular person to learn skiing – the balance, the coordination, the confidence. Now imagine doing it when you can't properly feel your feet because of the cold, and the other foot is artificial. At sub-zero temperatures, even putting on our skiing shoes and equipment became an ordeal that took twice as long as normal.

For those of us with amputations, there was another layer of complexity. If our "stump", the part of the leg that remained after amputation, got swollen from the extreme cold, or if the prosthetic didn't fit exactly right due to the temperature changes, it became incredibly painful and potentially risky. We had to be extra vigilant, checking and rechecking every piece of equipment, every fit, every sensation we could still feel.

On the very first day, we encountered what seemed to be an insurmountable practical problem. We went to the equipment storehouse to get our ski boots and gear, excitement and nervousness mixing in our hearts. The ski boots handed to us were exactly what you'd expect – hard, moulded plastic, rigid and unforgiving, designed for maximum control on the slopes.

The moment we saw those boots, a wave of concern washed over us. Our prosthetic feet, unlike real feet, have fixed ankles that don't bend or flex like natural joints. As we tried to put on the boots, the reality hit us hard, some of us simply couldn't get them on properly because the prosthetic ankle wouldn't bend to slide into the rigid boot structure.

For about an hour, we sat there in that cold storehouse, trying different approaches, different angles, growing more frustrated by the minute. It felt like we had travelled all this way, prepared mentally and emotionally for this challenge, only to be stopped by something as basic as putting on boots. The disappointment was palpable. Some of the boys started questioning whether this was even possible.

But giving up was not in our vocabulary. After much discussion and experimentation, we came up with a classic Indian "jugaad", we removed the inner liner of each ski boot, the soft padding inside that provides comfort. That small modification created just enough extra space to accommodate our prosthetic feet. It wasn't perfect, it wasn't comfortable, but it worked. And sometimes, that's all you need, a solution that works, no matter how unconventional.

With that small victory under our belts and our boots finally on, we moved to the practice area, a gentle slope where skiing beginners traditionally take their first tentative steps on snow. None of us had ever been on skis before, so we were truly starting from absolute zero, with the added challenge of our physical limitations.

The first lesson was humbling beyond words. Standing on skis turned out to be far more difficult than any of us had imagined. Within seconds of strapping on those long, slippery planks, we were all over the place, sliding, slipping, and tumbling into the snow like novices trying to walk on ice for the first time.

The falls were spectacular and frequent. We'd try to stand up straight, only to find ourselves sliding backward or sideways, arms flailing wildly as we tried to maintain our balance. Gowhair would fall and immediately burst into laughter, which would make the rest of us laugh even as we picked ourselves up from the snow. Abdul Rehman turned every fall into a joke, lightening the mood when frustration threatened to take over.

However, our instructors were patient angels. They had seen it all before, but perhaps never with a group quite like ours. We also had the constant support and encouragement of Major General R.K. Singh, who was personally overseeing our training. His presence meant everything to us. Here was a senior officer, taking time from his incredibly busy schedule, believing in us when we were struggling to believe in ourselves.

Under their expert guidance and with General R.K Singh's unwavering faith and constant motivation, we made a collective decision that would define the next three weeks: we would not retreat, we would not give up, no matter how hard it became, no matter how many times we fell.

Each day brought new lessons and new struggles. We learned the basics of skiing piece by piece, how to slide on snow without falling flat on our faces, how to stop ourselves using the "pizza" or snowplough technique (making a wedge shape with our skis), how to make turns without ending up as human snowballs, and most importantly, how to balance on those narrow strips of fibreglass while moving down a slope.

Every single day, we discovered new things about our own limitations, and more importantly, about our ability to push beyond them. The cold continued to bite into us relentlessly. Our muscles were constantly strained from the unfamiliar movements and the effort to maintain our balance. Mentally, it was exhausting to keep going when progress seemed painfully slow, when every small achievement was followed by another challenging hurdle.

The physical toll was immense. Sometimes, the stress and impact of falls would actually break a prosthetic leg, sending its owner tumbling head-first into the snow. These moments were particularly scary because a broken prosthetic meant not just a fall, but potentially being sidelined until repairs could be made.

Many of us developed painful blisters on our stumps where the prosthetic limbs attached, caused by the constant friction and movement during skiing. Every night, we would tend to those wounds, applying bandages and antiseptic, knowing we'd have to put on the same equipment the next morning and go through it all over again.

The mornings were consistently the most difficult part of each day. Waking up with sore muscles, seeing those blisters, feeling the weight of another day's challenges ahead of us, it would have been so easy to say, "today, I'll rest. Today, I'll sit this one out." But every single morning, after warming up and stretching, we would look at each other, take a collective deep breath, and gear up with complete commitment to face whatever the mountain would throw at us.

Slowly but surely, we began to improve. It wasn't dramatic or sudden, it was gradual, almost imperceptible at first. Maybe one less fall than the previous day. Maybe holding our balance for five seconds longer. Maybe making a turn without ending up in the snow. These small victories started adding up, building our confidence bit by bit.

The breakthrough came in the third week. These six young men, who just days before could barely stand upright on skis without support, successfully skied down a continuous stretch of about 250 metres without falling even once! When we measured the distance afterwards, we were amazed and over-whelmed with emotion. What had seemed absolutely impossible on day one had become our reality.

The scene at the bottom of that slope was unforgettable. We cheered, we hugged, some of us even cried with joy. That 250 metre skiing wasn't just distance covered on snow, it was proof of human determination, proof that with enough persistence and the right attitude, barriers that seem impossible can be broken.

Word of our progress began to spread beyond Gulmarg. Visitors, other trainees, even locals started talking about the group of specially-abled youngsters who were learning to ski. The story reached newspapers and social media. People who heard about it were inspired, amazed, and moved.

Many people had always said, "Skiing for the specially-abled is yet to be properly explored in India," and they were absolutely right, it wasn't common, it wasn't even considered possible by many. But here we were, not just exploring it but excelling in it, proving that with the right support, training, and most importantly, the right mindset, anything is achievable.

Through sheer courage, unwavering commitment, and that magical attitude of "So what", so what if we have disabilities, so what if it's difficult, so what if people doubt us, these boys shattered every preconceived notion about what differently-abled individuals can or cannot accomplish. They sent a resounding message to youth everywhere, especially in Kashmir, but really to the whole world: despite whatever adversities life throws your way, determination and hard work will always, eventually, be rewarded.

This entire experience brought something else

that was perhaps even more valuable than the skiing skills – hope. Hope for other specially-abled youth who might now believe that they too could take up skiing. Hope for parents who might now encourage their children to dream bigger. Some of these boys even started talking about representing India in the Paralympics for skiing one day! That spark of ambition, once lit, began to burn brighter with each passing day.

And that's what this story is truly about at its core. It's not just about learning to ski or conquering a slope in the Himalayas. It's about defying limitations that society places on you. It's about conquering fears that live inside your own mind. It's about inspiring not just yourself, but everyone who hears your story. It's about proving that any challenge, no matter how daunting, can be met with a smile, determination, and that powerful "So what" attitude.

By the end of those transformative three weeks, we had all changed in ways we couldn't have imagined. Yes, we learned how to ski, that was the obvious achievement. But more importantly, we proved something profound to ourselves and to everyone watching that a resilient human spirit can overcome even the most daunting hurdles that life presents.

In every fall we took and every time we got up, in every "So what if it's hard, let's try again" that we whispered to ourselves, we discovered the true meaning of determination and courage. We learned that limitations often exist more in our minds than in our bodies. We understood that the biggest victories come not from avoiding challenges, but from embracing them wholeheartedly.

And that, is the real triumph of our story, not just learning to ski, but learning to embrace any challenge with the spirit that's captured perfectly in those two simple yet powerful words: "So What."

CHAPTER XII

A COLLECTION OF LIFE'S BATTLE CRIES

As I bring this journey to its close, I want to share with you one final and crucial lesson, one that has carried me through every setback, every challenge, and every unexpected turn in life. It is the simple yet profound power of two words: "So what."

Life, as we've seen through these stories and experiences, is beautifully unpredictable. We all face obstacles, some small and some earth-shaking. Sometimes, it feels as if the weight of the world rests upon our shoulders. But the way we respond to these moments defines who we are. Are we defeated by fear, doubt, or disappointment? Or do we rise, shrug off the setbacks, and say with quiet strength, "So what?"

Let me lay out a collection of real-life "So what" responses. These are not just phrases, they are affirmations, battle cries, and reminders of the indomitable spirit within all of us. Each "So what" is a declaration that circumstances don't define destiny, resilience does. Feel it as you read.

The So What for Professional and Career Challenges

I lost my job – So What! I will find another one.

My business failed – So What! I will build it again.

I didn't get the promotion – So What! Life doesn't stop here.

I failed in my interview – So What! I will try again.

I was laid off from my dream job – So What! I will find an even better one that values me.

My start-up failed and I lost everything – So What! I will use this experience to build something even better.

My project was cancelled after months of work – So What! I gained valuable skills that no one can take away.

I was demoted due to company restructuring – So What! This is just a detour, not a dead end.

My business partner betrayed me – So What! I will rebuild it.

I am bullied at work by my colleagues – So What! Their behaviour reflects on them, not me.

I realized I wasted 10 years in the wrong career – So What! It's never too late to change direction.

The pandemic destroyed my business – So What! I will adapt and find new ways to keep moving.

The economy collapsed and took my industry with it – So What! I will develop new skills for the changing world.

The So What for Students: Academic and Learning Setbacks

I got less marks in class 11 – So What! I will study harder and improve.

I couldn't clear my JEE/NEET – So What! Life gives more opportunities. Don't stop!

I failed my exam – So What! I will prepare for the next one and pass with flying colours.

I wasn't accepted by the college I wanted – So What! Success comes from within, not institutions.

I failed the certification exam – So What! I will study smarter and pass next time.

I couldn't complete my doctorate – So What! I will refine my research and come back stronger.

My research paper was not accepted for publication – So What! I will revise and submit it elsewhere.

I dropped out of college due to financial constraints – So What! There are many other good ways to success.

I couldn't pass the Bar exam on my first attempt – So What! Many successful advocates needed multiple attempts.

I couldn't clear my SSB – So What! I will work on myself and try again.

This was my last attempt – So What! I will still make a better person.

I'm too old to learn new technology – So What! Nothing stops you. Age brings wisdom that complements new skills.

The So What for Financial and Economic Hardships

I lost money in investment – So What! It's okay, I will gain next time.

I'm facing retirement with no savings – So What! I will rebuild and work longer if necessary.

I couldn't afford my child's college tuition – So What! We will find scholarships and alternative paths.

My inheritance was stolen by a family member – So What! I will create my own wealth.

I lost everything in a natural disaster – So What! I still have my life and the ability to rebuild.

The So What for Social and Relationship Challenges

My girlfriend/boyfriend rejected me – So What! That doesn't make me a loser.

My classmates/colleagues hate me – So What! I regard myself no less.

I'm rejected by my team – So What! I will still keep going.

I got divorced – So What! I will rediscover who I am as an individual.

My new relationship is not working out – So What! That doesn't mean I am a failure.

My children don't want to speak to me – So What! I will work to heal our relationship with patience and love.

I was excluded from my friends group – So What! True friends wouldn't abandon me.

My family disowned me for my choices – So What! I will still not give up on relationships.

I was publicly humiliated on social media – So What! The opinions of strangers don't define my worth.

My best friend betrayed my trust – So What! Life still goes on.

I feel lonely – So What! I will use this solitude to build myself better.

Social media made me feel inadequate – So What! I will focus on real relationships and authentic living.

The So What for Personal Growth and Self-Discovery

I am a failure – So What! I will still try.

I have doubts about myself – So What! I will start writing and work on my strengths and weaknesses.

I am struggling to focus – So What! I will realign my mind.

I'm scared of failure – So What! It's part of the path to success.

I couldn't keep my resolution – So What! I will try again and stay committed.

I discovered I've been living a lie about myself – So What! Authenticity begins with honest self-awareness.

I found out my life's achievements meant nothing to me – So What! I will redefine what success means.

I realized I've been pleasing people all my life – So What! Now onwards I will learn to honour my own priorities.

I discovered I'm not as smart as I thought – So What! Wisdom comes from recognizing our limitations.

I feel completely lost and don't know my purpose – So What! The journey of discovery is itself purposeful.

Everyone doubts my abilities – So What! Self-belief is the only belief that truly matters.

I made mistakes that hurt people I love – So What! I will make amends and learn to do better.

The So What for Performance and Achievement Challenges

I missed my target – So What! I will set a new goal and work for it.

I faced rejection – So What! It doesn't mean the end of the world.

I lost an important match – So What! I will practise harder and win next time.

I'm not good at public speaking – So What! I will speak, let others laugh.

I don't have all the resources – So What! I will make the most of what I have.

I can't go on stage, people will judge me – So What! Let them judge!

I want to live but fear leaving my business – So

What! What's the point of building an empire if you're too sick to enjoy it? You're competing with ghosts while your life slips away. Stop the race, start living!

The So What for Age and Life Transitions

I'm 50 and starting over completely – So What! Experience is my greatest asset now.

I missed my chance to have the family I wanted – So What! I will find other ways to nurture and contribute.

I wasted my youth on the wrong pursuits – So What! Every day is a new opportunity to live meaningfully.

My dreams didn't come true by the age I planned – So What! Dreams don't have expiry dates.

I'm not where I thought I'd be at this age – So What! Life rarely follows the plans we make.

The So What for Social Judgement and External Pressures

People laugh at me – So What! I will also laugh with them!

I am facing criticism – So What! I will keep doing my work dedicatedly.

The So What for Everyday Challenges and Mindsets

It's raining – So What! I will continue walking or working.

Life knocked me down repeatedly – So What! Each time I get up, I'm stronger than before.

The world seems against me today – So What! I am my own greatest ally and that's enough.

It's all gone, I feel like giving up on everything – So What! Tomorrow might be the day everything changes.

The So What for Health and Physical Challenges

I was diagnosed with a chronic illness – So What! I will adapt and live my life to the fullest.

I had a heart attack at 35 – So What! I will use this as motivation to live healthier.

I became permanently disabled in an accident – So What! My spirit remains unbroken and my purpose unchanged.

I suffer from depression and anxiety – So What! I will seek help and fight this battle every day.

I have a learning disability – So What! I will find alternative ways to achieve my goals.

I lost my vision unexpectedly – So What! I will develop my other senses and abilities.

My cancer came back after remission – So What! I fought it before, and I will fight it again.

I was told I can't have children – So What! There are many ways to build a family and find purpose.

I admitted I have an addiction – So What! Acknowledging the problem is the first step to recovery.

I lost my leg – So What! I will come back again. And I came back too.

These "So what" responses are more than mere words, they represent an attitude that prepares you to face the situation which you always dreaded. It's a mindset shift from victimhood to victory, from fear to faith. When life knocks you down, this powerful phrase urges you to get back up, brush yourself off, and face what comes next with courage.

As I write these words, and as you read them at this very moment, somewhere on a desolate mountain peak and in a windswept valley, a soldier stands sentinel at a remote post in the harshest of conditions. Through blinding snow with frost on his breath, he stands unwavering and roars, "So what if I have to face this brutal weather? I will guard our frontiers. I will protect my people."

At this very instant, another brave soldier faces the deadly bullets, feeling the sting of shrapnel, watching his own blood stain. Yet in his pain, he finds the strength to say, "So what if I have to face these bullets? I will not let the enemy step onto our sacred soil."

And somewhere, perhaps in this very hour, in an operation, before a soldier draws his final breath in the line of duty, his last words, barely whispered yet thunderous in his meaning: "So what if it costs me my life? I will complete the mission. My sacrifice will not be in vain."

What's your next "So What!"